'even when I feel nothing, I feel it completely'

Sylvia Plath

Pesky Publishing Ltd
(SC768953)

www.peskypublishing.co.uk

ISBN 978-1-7396901-4-4

Design by mary@blackdoggraphics.co.uk.
All artwork is subject to copyright.

1st Edition

First Printed: 2024

Pesky Publishing Ltd (info@peskypublishing.co.uk)

www.peskypublishing.co.uk

A few words...

A close friend of mine suggested that we call this collection Poems for Poetry Refuseniks. They are mostly poems people can relate to - they are not intellectual, or abstract, or surreal. They are about life as most of us experience it, full of heartbreak, joy, anger, beauty and humour.

The section on the tragedy unfolding in Palestine is, admittedly, a lot darker. These poems have often been called 'powerful', but dark words are needed for dark times and silence is not an option.

One of the greatest compliments I ever received was when a woman I have never met reached out to me online and told me how my poem on grief had resonated with her, after the death of her son. Poetry is written both by and for the poet, to express a feeling, or capture a moment in time, and for the reader, to enjoy and interpret as they will. I do hope you find something in this collection that resonates.

Thanks to my many patient friends who have provided a not-entirely reluctant audience and thanks to the people in my life who inspired some of the sorrow and the happiness that has found its way onto these pages.

DANCING WITH ELLIE

Wild is the night where love dances,
Until the moon slides us into tomorrow

SEVILLE

In old Seville
we drifted,
aimless as a dream,
and all the world
lay for our taking,
tables squeezed
in cobbled squares
and plates of tapas,
spread for us,
were served
beneath a winter sky.

The bitter-orange streets
were gold
beneath our feet,
adrift between
the Moorish towers,
the glistening spires.
A backdrop to this conquered land.
You held my hand!

And time itself
relented for a day,
and slowed,
and held its breath for us
In old Seville.

EPIC

I loved you a tempest,
with forked silver lightning
I loved you a pale hunter's moon,
sailing high.

The star-spangled heavens,
an unchained Andromeda,
spread like a map
on an aubergine sky.

I dreamed you a kingdom
of forests and mountains,
with peacocks and parrots and
verdigris shores.

I dreamed you a palace
of rhinestones and rubies,
with courtyards and fountains
and wide-open doors.

I sculpted a temple
from moonbeams and madness,
with twelve ivory towers and
a high dreaming steeple.

But you chose a 3-bedroom semi,
with parking.
You cannot do epic shit
with basic people!

LOVE?

It was love, of a kind.

Not the kind you would drop, perhaps,
into a card to Aunt Hermione
Or that sits politely between the sofa
and the potted palm.
It didn't arrive by invitation,
all neatly pressed and clean and shiny.
No, it was never simple,
or convenient or calm.

It didn't come gift-wrapped
in layers of pretty pastel paper.
It was back door, off beat,
not at all the kind of love
you'd hoped to find.
It wasn't straight or set or square,
or boxed or packaged.
But still it was, I think,
love, of a kind.

WHEN

I came across a photo,
taken early,
before regret
had washed the laughter
into silence.
When all the world
was vivid as a
lover's gaze,
and passing planes
wrote haiku
across a china sky.
I came across a message
sent in haste,
from a dawn-hushed doorstep
in another time.
As ripe as summer
and as warm with promise
as the oranges
that glowed
on laden branches
behind your outspread arms.

I deleted
both the photo
and the text...
but only from my phone.

CRUMBS

Crumbs from your table
sweet and addictive
'All I can spare'
I hear you call.
But here, on the underside,
feels restrictive.
A place AT your table
or not at all.

I NEVER SEE IT COMING

I never see it coming,
that moment when everything falls apart.
Like a tower block, crashing,
leaving me alive,
but shell-shocked
in the aftermath.
And then I try to fix it.
Scrabbling at the rubble with my bare hands,
looking for survivors,
a sign of life,
trying for damage limitation
on a DNR.
When the smoke has lifted,
some months later, when the air has cleared,
I look back and realise,
it was over then.
That exact moment
I just didn't see it coming.

EMPTY

Empty as a paper bag
blown into a corner
by yesterday's wind.
Empty as a station,
when the last train leaves
and the lights are dimmed.
Where dry leaves huddle
in forgotten piles,
and pigeons sleep
and the lonely stars
shine dimly,
and the watchers keep.
Empty as a promise,
barely made or meant
and soon forgotten.
Empty as a windfall peach,
smooth skinned and dusky-sweet
but rotten.
Empty as the darkness,
where love danced,
until the fickle moon
tired of love and dance,
and song
and called our tune.

DOG

Wouldn't it be great if love was a dog?
It would do what you wanted
and walk at your heel.
Wouldn't it be cool if love was a canine?
You could buy it a leash
and control how you feel.
It would come when you called it,
and jump when you told it,
and go when you asked it,
and stop on command.
It would fetch, it would carry,
and faithfully dally,
and do all the things
that your heart may demand.
It would play it your way
it would sit, it would stay,
it would leave when you left,
and fit in with your timeline .
It would quiet at a word
and then never be heard.
How easy would love be
if it was a canine?

CAT

It cannot be commanded,
it arrives at will.
It will not heel, or heed you,
or move, or still.
It cannot be persuaded
or told to go,
or stay, or stop, or alter,
or pause, or slow.
It cannot be reordered
or quite understood.
Inscrutable, immutable,
for worse, for good,
it will fool you, bewitch you,
evade you, withdraw.
It will woo you with rapture,
and wound you with claw,
it will lie where it will,
it will leave in the night,
it will never obey you,
it's despair, it's delight.
It defies, it dictates,
takes you high, leaves you flat.
Breaks your heart without blinking -
I think love is a cat.

HEART

Harden your heart
or she will break it,
like a tinsel toy
wrapped casually
around careless fingers.

Harden your heart
or when she drops it,
it will shatter.
Better it bounce
and roll away.

Harden your heart
or redirect it.
no matter.
it is no longer yours
to give.

PALESTINE

It didn't happen overnight, it was a gradual process.
It's not as if I woke at cockcrow to a diminished
station.
He didn't arrive with wrecking ball and trebuchet.
It was a much more surreptitious demolition.

A border terrier pissed up the fence and waited.
The boundaries squeezed, the settler staked his claim.
That, which I'm told would never come between us,
Became a wall, in everything but name.

I vanished! Right before my very eyes,
I vanished.
Depleted, as my sands ran slowly out of time.
Displaced, I'm dispossessed; abandoned, scattered.
Broken hearted. - I am Palestine.

HAIKU

clouds, plump as hippos
wallow in a muddied sky
contemplating rain

wind in the shutters
seeking company
tired of leafless trees

in the face of horror
still the unbroken wonder
of love

peace, like summer sun,
taken for granted until
winter comes howling

a child's toy, armless
lies in the rubble, wishing
we were all unarmed

old pond
I jump, unknowing
prince or frog?

divided by their faiths,
implacable in enmity,
united in their grief

voices of old gods
a whisper among
the banana palms

full moon over Rafah
bears silent witness
perhaps its silence explains
why it is allowed

you and me darling
it is written in the stars
I know. I wrote it.

how much longing
is contained within the card
I dare not send?

a small seed of hope
I over watered it

early morning sun
slides up your bed to wake you
how I envy it

we travel with a
backpack full of memories
and a pocket full of dreams

bad deeds like litter
dropped into our oceans
wash up upon our shores

cat lies, curled
content in her own completeness
how I envy her

defiant feet, unbidden
take me still to the place
where hope lies buried

to me you were home,
where my heart returned at night
but you changed the locks.

small bodies, broken
identified only by names
scrawled on tiny palms

blown into corners,
yesterday's litter joins
the homeless where they sleep

her fat floral arse
the deckchair groans on impact
the brass band plays on

DARTMOOR IN 4 SEASONS

ablaze with colour
trees in their party dresses
dancing in the breeze

following a leat
through ancient woodlands
dreaming of forgotten summers

a line of willows
drops gold into the river
old love letters

a five-bar gate
jammed open in the knee-high drifts
helpless against the snow

OUT OF EDEN

BROKEN

I broke my leg.
They stuck it back together
with a metal rod, and stitches,
and, in time I learned to walk again.
But never with the same panache
and still, at times, it falters,
or wakes me, aching, in the night.

You broke my heart.
I stuck it back together
with a grief that felt like drowning,
and, in time, I learned to live again.
But never with the same panache
and often, still, it falters,
or wakes me, aching, in the night.

If either were to break again,
my leg would better take the pain.

SQUIRRELS IN MY ATTIC

Grief slid in through the crack in my heart
left by your passing,
when everything I trusted, failed.
When promises I'd harvested
and stored against a rainy day,
like wheat, stacked for the winter,
turned to chaff.

Grief moved in and set up home.
Like mice, nesting
in the void in my walls,
in the empty spaces,
in the darkness.
Or thundering overhead
at unseemly hours
roughshod and heedless,
like squirrels in my attic.

Grief moved in, in a staged procession,
sparring for a while with hope and disbelief
Now it has changed the locks
and put up curtains.

Everything outside my window
looks the same.
The winter tree still hangs her
naked branches against the silver sky.
Rooks still swirl and shout into the dusk
each evening
And lights still glow in neighbours' windows.
But I have squirrels in my attic.

UNSURFED

all my passion
all of my depth
perfect waves
that broke unsurfed
upon the shore
of your cowardice
leaving sea foam
wind blown
like the confetti
from some suburban wedding
unconsummated
while the guests
choked on cheap spumante
eating ice cream
from plastic spoons

I am the wind
I am the concerto
played to deaf ears
I am the unpicked apple
Eve rejected
fearing censure
I am the unfinished novel
I am the unlit beacon
I am the dance
you sat out
I am the blood red dress
worn proudly
among the mourners
at the death
of love

TERMINOLOGY

She said:
'I love you dearly',
but she meant:
'a certain fondness'.

She said:
'You will always be my darling',
but she meant:
'Just for a while'.

I said:
'I love you deeply'
and I meant:
'With every heartbeat'

I said:
'You will always be my treasure'
and I meant:
'Til worlds collide'.

She said:
'Let's take it gently'
but she meant:
'Let's keep our distance'.

I said:
'My heart is your heart'.

Only one of us lied.

COBWEB

I watched the raindrops fall
upon the hawthorn
and busied myself with counting
the spider strands,
those captured beads
like little silver fish,
wet and gleaming.
And for that moment
quite forgot.
Until the breeze picked up
and once again, tugged at my sleeve.
Denying my forgetting,
Whispering your name.

UNFINISHED NOVEL

You galloped through to chapter ten,
devouring every page with eager joy
Somewhere in the middle of eleven
your focus shifted.
Picked up and dropped again
a few more times.
Now, dog-eared and dusty, I lie,
discarded on the pile
of your regrets.

SNOW

If snow falls this Christmas
Will you gaze out upon your winter garden
and smile?
Will you sit up in bed
Feeding biscuits to the dog,
And delay a while,
Watching the swirling flakes
Tumble silently out of
This same sky?
Will the drift
Stack up on your early morning doorstep
And stay?
Will you pull on your boots,
Let the animals, unthinking,
Into this new, white day?
Or pause, and remember,
just for a moment,
We are still
Under this same sky.

THE PRINCESS DIARIES

(poems dictated by my cat)

'So, this puppy shit – why d'ya do it -
I thought I was all you needed?'
I say, 'I thought it would stop the pain'.
She swishes her tail.
'Really?'
I say, 'probably not'.
She feeds me a look
I feed her cat cocaine
Neither of us know where the puppy is
we should be minding,
we just carry on sitting outside
in the rain.

DREAMING OF WAKING

Dreaming of waking
waking in my quiet bedroom
overlooking the banana palms
slatted light seeping in
through old wooden shutters
half the room alight
half in shadow
a metaphor perhaps?
outside
the early baby dragons
huff and puff
and exhale flame
as they drift through
the palm trees
dragging their baskets
towards the Nile
the call to prayer
follows them
across a pale blue
papyrus sky

dreaming of waking
in my quiet bedroom

or wishing?

CLOSE ENCOUNTER

I saw you today
quite unexpectedly

It was a shock to recognise
that you are now a stranger
the familiar shape of your body
now a foreign land
to which I have no visa
the hands that I once held
no longer open.

I saw you today
Quite by chance
I dont think you saw me
Just brushed past

Almost
Close enough to touch.

OTHER STUFF

TREE

Outside my morning window
the familiar shape.
Its bare bones strangely beautiful
against an ice blue sky.
Sun clings to it,
puddles in its branches,
like a pool of light
on an empty stage
waiting for the story to unfold.

CLOUDS OVER DARTMOOR

A hole in the heavens through which hope bleeds,
ripped apart by hate and violence.
Or maybe a door through which light feeds
a lull, the calm, the grace of silence.
The same sky over all our heads
yet one drops hatred death and terror.
The worst I can expect from mine
is rain -
and I have an umbrella.

OWL

Night closes softly, over still- warm hills,
creeping into valleys where the hamlets hide.
Leaching light from stony fields,
sheep, half-dimmed in the fading light.
Quietly swallowing lanes and houses.
Seeping into farms and evening meadows,
where dogs guard cattle, milked of light,
and trees surrender into shadow.
A tired sun dips over the horizon,
a last, late blackbird spills a chord into the night.
Yellow lamps leap to life in cottage windows
And owl takes flight.

PIGEONS

Beneath the old bridge
pigeons roost, in alcoves,
cooing warning as we pass beneath.
Upon your own heads be it.

SHEEP BY BRENTOR

White sheep,
bleeding from their ink-wounds,
spill
like scattered paper bags,
windswept, all across the dappled hills
of Dartmoor,
where, above the heather line,
washed watercolour by the rain,
where twilight and the sky align
in silence, stands Brentor.

Thunder fades to memory
and lightning leaves the ripening sky
where remnants of the white-pink tails
of mares are tethered out to dry.
And foals, in leggy wonder race
the autumn shadows on the hill.
A sulky sun turns pink, then gold
The last sheep, sleep
And all is still.

MAGPIE

Magpie bursts from a hawthorn tree,
pied as a piper, colours three.
Calls to the children 'come with me',
a reckoning for parsimony.

All that glitters is not real.
All I stole was there to steal.
Used as an empty cotton reel.
Nothing left to mend or feel.

Magpie bursts from a hawthorn tree
Steals the fledglings, one, two, three.
Oh, but the eggs lie still for me
I'll take and bake a mystery.

Over the hill and faraway
we danced until the end of day.
Happy to be led astray,
and heedless of the price to pay.

MODERN MANHOOD

Modern Man is dispossessed
of all his Grandsire's Manly Traits.
The bread now won by female labour,
girls no longer need a saviour.
Chargers are no longer white,
but multi-coloured, rainbow bright.
Blue stockings walk the Halls of Power,
no longer mocked as 'too highbrow'.

A modern maiden calls the shots,
she writes the scripts, directs the plots.
An offered seat meets female scorn,
well- mannered men are left, forlorn,
unsure which path they now should tread.
At work! At home! Abroad! In bed!
But one advantage god still grants,
although she took away your lance,
though you no longer Alpha be,
at least you need not Sit to Pee.

LIT CRIT

I had a dream
that I was Dead and Famous
(usually a compelling mix)
And my poems so renowned
they were taught in school,
force-fed to listless children,
tired of other people's musing
The teacher read:
'The ghost of yesterday
blew in like a banshee
riding eastern winds,
chilling my very bones',
while kids on stealthy phones
under their desks
read stuff of their own choosing

'Apparently',
she explained,
'this was a metaphor
for regional unrest
and the rekindling of
old grievances,
blown in on the wind
of a new- era cold -war.'
But what if
I simply meant
what I said?
That it was bloody cold
I was chilled to the bone,
and I see dead people?
Just that
And nothing more?

WRITING ON THE WALL

Love is wast (sic) of time
The writing's on the wall
But ah what a time it was
The best of all.

JAR

We took the pebbles
from the river beach,
wet and shiny
as little fish,
smooth and warm
from borrowed sun.

Pockets full of sand,
we counted them.
A stone for every day,
into an old, cracked jar.
Filled with endless summer.
All our dreams.

We removed them,
one by one.
until there were none.

BOOK ON THE BUS

I left my book on the Number Ten.
Put it down to jig my winter clothing,
scarf wrapped tight
to keep my head straight.
Balance has become a problem
since the world lost its bearings.

I left my book on the Number Ten.
Put it down while I rang the bell.
I hadn't even got to the part
where she marries him.
Just as well.
Maybe I saved her
from herself.

I left my book on the Number Ten.
Put it down while I zipped my jacket.
I never got it back again.
Perhaps some stories
Are best left unfinished.
Left with the possibility
At least
of a happy ending.

IS THERE A PLACE

Is there a place that haunts you still,
in some abandoned slot in time?
Where caught in amber, fossilized,
a younger you still dreams, still sighs?

Do shadows play, as they were wont
to do, along the mellow walls?
Do tractors hum in distant fields?
Do horses stamp in hay-strewn stalls?

The shadow of a memory.
Your foot upon the flagstone floor
And would my heart still leap to hear
your hand upon the kitchen door?

And if I went there, would I find
the sun still smiles from mirror skies?
That same, still summer, heavy,
with the smell of fruit, the buzz of flies.

And muffled in the opium air
the clop of hooves in heavy dust.
A blond lunged his horse –
Oh, would I find it still, or is it just

An empty orchard, broken down
the apples trees all gone to seed.
And fruit, unheeded, rotting
by a broken gate among the weeds.

And would I run through tangled grass,
to Bidlake, sleeping in the sun?
Or would I find it overgrown,
the blond boy, you, the horses - gone?

CROW

Let us swallow Hope
before it takes root.
Let us choose Now
over all the tomorrows.
Let us cook and devour
the golden goose.
Instead of investing,
borrow.
Gobble up the seed
before it grows
Eden to Armageddon
A feast for crows.

DAYS

Days lay spread before me,
like a pile of ribboned gifts.
The promise of pleasure
in abundance,
too many days to measure,
stretching as far
as the eye could see.

But, little by little,
days trickled away
by the back door,
through the windows.
At first, barely noticed
but soon, knocking, knocking.
Calling Time.

Now I sit with suitcase packed,
the last minute squeezed
from the last hour.
The last sunset,
The last goodbye.

All those days
that spread before me,
like Christmas chocolates
waiting to be opened.
I have eaten them all.

YOUNG

Young
The place we once lived
where everything was possible
we thought it was a country
attached to the world
by endless opportunity
We thought we were
the first explorers
We thought everything
was ours, and new
Only later
and not as much later
as you may imagine
we discovered that
Young
is not a forever home.
Or even a long layover.
It is an express train
hurtling into tomorrow
with no station stops.

WAR AND POLITICS

BEFORE YOU JUDGE

Fully immerse yourself
in a life which you do not own,
not even the water you drink,
or the sky above your head.
Fully immerse yourself
in the land where you belong,
that offers no belonging,
where you were born and raised and bred.

A land, embargoed,
blockaded, vilified, exhausted.
Where you are neither granted leave to stay
nor allowed to ever leave.
Live, trapped among the rubble
of this land you may not leave,
this bombsite of stolen ambitions,
this ignominy without reprieve.

Fully immerse yourself
in a land where hope is hopeless,
where your scream is met by silence
and every wish will be declined.
Live, trapped, dispossessed,
despised, occupied, tormented
fully for just one day -
and then judge Palestine.

POSSESSION

Possession,
being nine tenths of the law,
needs a little consideration.
Along with the issues, perhaps,
of addition
and subtraction.

Take, for example:
'we should be looking after
(our own) people first'

Simple subtraction
changes racist rhetoric
into philanthropic
abstraction.

AT GOD'S GATE

I do not believe in any gods.
I believe in self determination.
I do not bow to some outdated dogma
with archaic laws, lost, largely, in translation

I do not select which lives most matter
based on colour, background, race or creed.
As far as I see it
Genocide is genocide. Greed is greed

No people are the chosen people.
No land historically god-given.
War has no faith, no justification, no 'right'
It is man-greed made and man-greed driven.

But if I had a smidgeon of faith
even in a tiny corner of my mind
I'd wonder how absolution could be given
for the annihilation of Palestine.

VALENTINE'S DAY

A million blood-red roses
for Palestine.
Keep the card you bought me
in its cellophane wrapping.
Take the love you offer
and share it with the abandoned.

Let's make Love platonic.
Secular.
Colour blind.
Make it matter.
Take the love you offer
on a plastic platter
and turn it into
bread and fishes.
Or water
for the dying.

Take the love you offer
and share it with the broken.
I do not need your love
if it comes from
A barren heart.

TORY BOT

Easy to spot a Tory-bot
they rally to the cause,
and greet the stain of Greed and Gain
with rapturous applause.

Material wealth in any form
is really all that matters
even when pursuit of it
leaves decency in tatters.

Oh they will sigh, ignore, deny
whatever may arise,
the dodgy deals, the daily steals,
the countless, blatant lies.

They blame the left, the past, the dead!
Blame Europe! Blame the war.
Blame immigrants, blame Corbyn.
Blame the liberals, blame the poor.

A Tory-bot, no doubt will say,
that sewage smells quite sweet.
And homeless people just a messy nuisance
on the street

And gross corruption in the corridors
of power is fine
And if the poor insist on being poor,
their fault, not mine!

Easy to spot a Tory-bot,
their blindness quickly shows.
They are the ones who will not see
the emperor has no clothes!

THE HATE GARDEN

Build a garden
from the rubble of a city.
Plant the seeds of hate.
Water it with the blood
of children.
Electrify the gate.

Blockade it all
with bars of propaganda.
Fence it in with guns.
Fertilise it with the bones
of fathers, mothers
daughters, sons.

Rip out the weeds
of hope and resistance,
the soil itself must weep.
Now hatred flowers
a thousand times .
You sowed, so will you reap.

DEVIL'S WORK

The devil woke on New Year's Day
with quiet satisfaction
Much of the work of yesteryear
was turning into action.
The hate dripped in
to souls of men
was permeating nicely,
the seeds of horror scattered
had been distributed wisely .

Evil triumphs everywhere
when Self diverts the masses .
Chuck in a bit of festive cheer,
distract the working classes.
Cloak it in fake piety
and wrap it up in glitter,
and while they glut on Christmas fare
throw Good out with the litter.

Atrocities are carried out
behind the Christmas story,
babies, buried in the rubble
sing of god in glory,
while men with hearts
as hard as ice
pump bullets into children,
shells delivered smack on time.
with love
from Uncle Biden.

The devil sat back on New Year's day
in quiet satisfaction
Nothing quite to start the year
like corrupt politicians.
Leaders with their bloodied hands
all bought and paid in shekels,
and nice new laws to close down
any soul who dares to heckle,

STOP

Stop whitewashing the news,
It's one jump short of lying.
Why talk of 'deepening crisis'
when there are thousands dying?
Why talk of 'right to defend'
when it masks such horror.
Try 'murdering little children'
let's make it clearer.
Don't talk of 'corridors of aid'
when they have no water.
Nothing to wash the blood and dust
from murdered sons and daughters
Dont talk of 'Israeli airstrikes'
talk of screaming, maimed, dismembered.
Talk of people trapped and helpless,
with no option of surrender.
Stop hiding behind religion
the gods have left this desperate place.
Let's say it how it is.
Greed. Hatred. Genocide. Race.
A thousand eyes for a Jewish eye
No hope of absolution.
Shooting fish in a bloodied barrel.
The final solution.

STARDUST

Why do you hate us?
We are made of stardust,
just like you.
If you prick us,
do we not bleed?
If you poison us
do we not die?

It comes from where.
this biblical hatred?
Through the centuries
we have hidden in ghettos,
worn our star of shame.
Buried ourselves in mass graves.

Why do you hate us?
The lands of your Fathers were ours to steal.
We buried your sons and daughters
beneath the rubble of genocide
in righteous vengeance.

We mocked your hunger.
Celebrated your pain.
We dispossessed you,
and we bombed you
as you fled.
We smashed the edifices
of your culture to dust.

We are stardust.
We are the chosen.
Why do you hate us?

KILL ME

If you bomb me,
Kill me.
Do not leave me, mangled,
bleeding out, in the street,
while you pose for selfies
and celebrate
your heroic deeds.

If you bomb me,
Kill me.
Do not send me to the hospital
with no doctors
with no roof.
To saw my leg off,
as I drown in my own blood.

If you bomb me,
Kill me.
Do not leave me whole,
to cradle my dead children
In my arms
and bury my Mother
in the mass grave that was Gaza.

If you bomb me,
Kill me
Do not bury me in the rubble
to die slowly
In the crushing darkness
Choking on bombdust
and my own screams.

We are seeds
Bury us, we will grow
Crush us,
we will take root
Burn us,
we will strengthen.
Spread us to the very winds
we will regroup.

If you bomb me,
Kill me.

THE LONGEST NIGHT

Bomb the Fifth Estate
Into oblivion.
Evil with impunity,
under cover of the longest night.
Build settlements upon its ashes
all along the Gaza strip.
Mushrooms spring from the rubble.
Pay nothing now
for a Villa by the sea!

Remember what Amalek has done to you.

Go, kill the ravens.
Tune the airways to our hymn sheet
and sing from it alone.
We are the Chosen People.
This is our bloodied land.
Founded on the crushed skulls of children,
let us build our Sunset Boulevard
atop a graveyard of humanity.

SUMMER 24

STUFF

Declutter,
it's good for the soul.
I bag up
a load of things
no longer needed.
Or past their best
(like me)
The hardly worn outfits
I promise myself will fit again,
The unused exercise machine
(another broken promise)
The faded curtains

Talking of broken promises
I find your letters
in a pile.
I really meant to bin them
But never quite.
The necklace you gave me
from Peru
You left it in my keeping
As I left my heart in yours
('I will treasure it' you told me)
I still sense you on it.

Sprigs of lavender
in the linen chest.
The replica bedouin pistol
insisted on by an eight year old,
twenty holidays ago
A well-loved jumper
that smells, still,
of pine woods and the sea.
A jewellery box
with broken hinges
All these links in a chain
to another time.

I separate them
to go, to keep.
The second pile grows bigger.
If souls reside within
the hearts of forests,
do memories actually live
within these faded treasures?

WHO WE LOVE

Who we love
is no one's business
but our own
no labels, please,
no colour coding,
no use-by date

bodies do not
run out of longing
as they age,
hearts do not
forget how to love.
souls do not
wither meekly
into loneliness,
without reaching
for the light

yes, it would be
convenient
to box us up
and put us on the shelf,
tidily stacked away
waiting only
for the flick of a duster
before we head
into the final night

but do not tell us
who to love
it is not a game of
paint by numbers
we are not horses
to be matched by height
or shade.
our hearts, our bodies
moments of connection
nobody's business
but our own.

ICE CREAM LOVE

What is love?
What do we mean by it?
I mean 'limitless'.
You mean 'quite a bit'.
Should be different words
This 'love' is confusing.
Do you love me
like you love your cat?
What word should we
be using?
Mild affection?
Or the sack of Troy?
Planets colliding?
Or a phase to enjoy?
Love that ice cream
Watch it melt
Guess that's how
you always felt.

UNDER CONSIDERATION

I asked the dead child;
'What is happening here?
Should we refer to it as genocide?
or just the plausibility of genocide?
The shell, signed by Uncle Sam,
was it 'unreasonable force'
when it blew you into
a dozen pieces?
Or just Israel's
Right to Self Defence?'

There was no answer
from her lifeless body
Or, at least,
the parts of it that I could find.

So, I asked the Mother,
howling her pain
over a skeletal child
dying slowly in her arms.
'Do you think this is famine?
Or just the threshold of famine?'
Her unseeing eyes
gave no response,
so I pressed her further.
'Do you condemn Hamas?
DO you condemn Hamas?"
There was no reply.
Just the steady thunder
of artillery fire,
half a mile away.

I asked the old man,
wheeling his legless son
between the rubble
and the bomb holes
on a hand pushed cart;
'Is this organised evacuation,
or further displacement?'
He stopped, as the meagre pile
of his remaining possessions
slid from the cart onto
the pitted road.
He waved an emaciated hand
at the ravaged land,
at the crater beside us,
where a village once stood.
'This is where they send us'
he said.

I asked the doctor,
fleeing from the hospital under fire,
carrying an infant
with tubes still protruding
from beneath its shroud;
'Is this where Hamas hides,
beneath this building?
Is this a war against terror?
Or is it ethnic cleansing
on a massive scale?'
'Fuck off with your terminology"
he shouted
Just before a sniper took him down.

Let's discuss it some more tomorrow.
I think the verdict remains 'unproven'.

THE PROMISED LAND

We are all nomads,
made of stardust,
seeking a home.
Wanton creepers in
nameless forests,
settlers in an
unknown future.
Scattered seeds
among the ruins
of yesterday
and the hope
of tomorrow.
Owning nothing.
Our birthright
the postcode
where our seedpod
cracked.
Travellers in time
and fortune,
Bound together
by the same cosmic laws
Separate
Alone
Apart
Colour coded,
for fast track
or failure
We are all nomads.

PRIDE

To Alan Turing, with gratitude and regret

A rainbow arcs across
a pale Home Counties sky,
where rows of manicured lawns
march in orderly procession,
and perfect Windsor knots
tie their owners together
in unspoken bonds
of frigid respectability

Here he was formed,
A product of the very England
that devoured its saviour.
Hounded to death by laws
without humanity.
That tied a perfect Windsor knot
in a stranglehold
around how many thousand necks?

We have pardoned him?
We, who owe him everything?
How will we ever pardon
Ourselves?
Lay a rainbow of flowers
For the lost
And beg forgiveness.

HONOURING THE DEAD

All this banging on
about remembering them.
Do you think
the shit-scared kid
with half his face
shot away,
dying in a place
he couldn't even name,
cared a toss about
a bloody wreath?
Or wondered if people
would march in silence,
80 years later?
Or gather in hushed solemnity
to lay flowers
on the beach?

Did the mothers nod their heads
when the telegrams came,
and say, consolingly
to each other,
'my lost boy
will be immortalised
in pomp and circumstance'
Did our glorious dead
hold their weeping women,
or unmet children,
even in their dreams?

Lest we forget?
How about we remember?
Remember the lesson we pledged
to learn. Never again
Stop celebrating our lost generation
and erecting plaques
to their noble sacrifices,
There is nothing noble
about dying in a foreign field
choking on your own terror
soaked in your own urine.

The only fitting tribute
to those from who we stole
their golden years,
is to put aside our enmities,
chain up the dogs of war.
Still the sounds of gunfire
and stem the flow of violence.
No amount of pious posturing
means anything
if we are doing it, still,
even as we pray.

HAIKU-TIME

precious moments
like water, trickle
through our fingers

yesterday's regrets
tomorrow's promises
suspended between

happiness
the turquoise flash
of a kingfisher

a moment in time
caught in a photograph
gone in a heartbeat

all the ghosts
of my past selves
walk behind me

sleepless nights
the ghosts of murdered children
whisper to me

broken fingers
tapping at my window pain
calling my name

always the same question
why did the world look away
while we were burning

FOR J

Words whizz around the room,
  like bats at dusk
    Some land near me,
      Some echo in far corners...
    Some crash and die.

    Some, I guess at,
And smile and nod.
      By other's eyebrows
        I know when I have guessed
      Inappropriately.

A ghost at the feast.
    Part of it,
        Yet, apart from it.
    Under the table,
          I take comfort in words
              on my phone .

Thanks to Rosie Dobbie (SWMBO) for exemplary and patient proof-reading and to Gillian Capel for ploughing through what must have seemed
like a poem a day, day after day.

Cover image, with thanks to Lucinda, Adrian and Katie Phillips. This is a photograph of the old trilho mounted on the wall at their house in Reriz, Portugal.

*Trilho - an agricultural utensil used
to thresh cereals on the threshing floor.*

All royalties from this book will be donated to various charities addressing the desperate plight of the people of Gaza.

If you wish to make your own donation,
recommended charities include:
MAP - map.org.uk
UNWRA - unwra.org.

9 781739 690144